The Ultimate Monthly Bill Ledger for Busy People

Activinotes

DAILY JOURNALS, PLANNERS, NOTEBOOKS AND OTHER BLANK BOOKS

Name: ....

Address: ....

E-mail : ....

Contact no's : ....

....

Month_____

Bills

INCOME
RENT
GAS
GROCERIES
LEFT FOR BILLS

EXPENSE	DUE	AMOUNT	PAID	BALANCE LEFT

NOTES
....
....
....
....

Month_____

Bills

INCOME
RENT
GAS
GROCERIES
LEFT FOR BILLS

EXPENSE	DUE	AMOUNT	PAID	BALANCE LEFT

NOTES

....

....

....

....

MONTH OF

Mon	Tue	Wed	Thurs	Fri	Sat	Sun

TO DO LIST

School	Home

★ _____   ★ _____

★ _____   ★ _____

★ _____   ★ _____

★ _____   ★ _____

Schedule

M	T	W	TH	F	S	S

Materials to Prepare
- _____
- _____
- _____
- _____
- _____

Email/Calls/Follow-Up
- _____
- _____
- _____
- _____
- _____

Reminders
- _____
- _____
- _____
- _____
- _____

Errands/Home/Personal
- _____
- _____
- _____
- _____
- _____
- _____

Upcoming To Do
- _____
- _____
- _____
- _____
- _____
- _____

Notes
- _____
- _____
- _____
- _____
- _____
- _____

Month_____

Bills

INCOME
RENT
GAS
GROCERIES
LEFT FOR BILLS

EXPENSE	DUE	AMOUNT	PAID	BALANCE LEFT

NOTES

....
....
....
....

Month_____

Bills

INCOME
RENT
GAS
GROCERIES
LEFT FOR BILLS

EXPENSE	DUE	AMOUNT	PAID	BALANCE LEFT

NOTES

....

....

....

....

MONTH OF

Mon	Tue	Wed	Thurs	Fri	Sat	Sun

TO DO LIST

School	Home

★ _____   ★ _____

★ _____   ★ _____

★ _____   ★ _____

★ _____   ★ _____

Schedule

M	**T**	**W**	**TH**	**F**	**S**	**S**

Materials to Prepare
- _____
- _____
- _____
- _____
- _____

Email/Calls/Follow-Up
- _____
- _____
- _____
- _____
- _____

Reminders
- _____
- _____
- _____
- _____
- _____

Errands/Home/Personal
- _____
- _____
- _____
- _____
- _____
- _____

Upcoming To Do
- _____
- _____
- _____
- _____
- _____
- _____

Notes
- _____
- _____
- _____
- _____
- _____
- _____

Month_____

Bills

INCOME
RENT
GAS
GROCERIES
LEFT FOR BILLS

EXPENSE	DUE	AMOUNT	PAID	BALANCE LEFT

NOTES

....
....
....
....

Month_____

Bills

INCOME
RENT
GAS
GROCERIES
LEFT FOR BILLS

EXPENSE	DUE	AMOUNT	PAID	BALANCE LEFT

NOTES

....
....
....
....

MONTH OF

Mon	Tue	Wed	Thurs	Fri	Sat	Sun

TO DO LIST

School	Home

★ _____   ★ _____

★ _____   ★ _____

★ _____   ★ _____

★ _____   ★ _____

Schedule

M	T	W	TH	F	S	S

Materials to Prepare
- _____
- _____
- _____
- _____
- _____

Email/Calls/Follow-Up
- _____
- _____
- _____
- _____
- _____

Reminders
- _____
- _____
- _____
- _____
- _____

Errands/Home/Personal
- _____
- _____
- _____
- _____
- _____
- _____

Upcoming To Do
- _____
- _____
- _____
- _____
- _____
- _____

Notes
- _____
- _____
- _____
- _____
- _____
- _____

Month_____

Bills

INCOME
RENT
GAS
GROCERIES
LEFT FOR BILLS

EXPENSE	DUE	AMOUNT	PAID	BALANCE LEFT

NOTES

....

....

....

....

Month_____

Bills

INCOME
RENT
GAS
GROCERIES
LEFT FOR BILLS

EXPENSE	DUE	AMOUNT	PAID	BALANCE LEFT

NOTES

....

....

....

....

MONTH OF

Mon	Tue	Wed	Thurs	Fri	Sat	Sun

TO DO LIST

School	Home

★ _____   ★ _____

★ _____   ★ _____

★ _____   ★ _____

★ _____   ★ _____

Schedule

M	**T**	**W**	**TH**	**F**	**S**	**S**

Materials to Prepare
- _____
- _____
- _____
- _____
- _____

Email/Calls/Follow-Up
- _____
- _____
- _____
- _____
- _____

Reminders
- _____
- _____
- _____
- _____
- _____

Errands/Home/Personal
- _____
- _____
- _____
- _____
- _____
- _____

Upcoming To Do
- _____
- _____
- _____
- _____
- _____
- _____

Notes
- _____
- _____
- _____
- _____
- _____
- _____

Month_____

Bills

INCOME
RENT
GAS
GROCERIES
LEFT FOR BILLS

EXPENSE	DUE	AMOUNT	PAID	BALANCE LEFT

NOTES

....
....
....
....

Month_____

Bills

INCOME
RENT
GAS
GROCERIES
LEFT FOR BILLS

EXPENSE	DUE	AMOUNT	PAID	BALANCE LEFT

NOTES

MONTH OF

Mon	Tue	Wed	Thurs	Fri	Sat	Sun

TO DO LIST

School	Home

★ _____   ★ _____

★ _____   ★ _____

★ _____   ★ _____

★ _____   ★ _____

Schedule

M	T	W	TH	F	S	S

Materials to Prepare
- _____
- _____
- _____
- _____
- _____

Email/Calls/Follow-Up
- _____
- _____
- _____
- _____
- _____

Reminders
- _____
- _____
- _____
- _____
- _____

Errands/Home/Personal
- _____
- _____
- _____
- _____
- _____
- _____

Upcoming To Do
- _____
- _____
- _____
- _____
- _____
- _____

Notes
- _____
- _____
- _____
- _____
- _____
- _____

Month_____

Bills

INCOME
RENT
GAS
GROCERIES
LEFT FOR BILLS

EXPENSE	DUE	AMOUNT	PAID	BALANCE LEFT

NOTES

....
....
....
....

Month_____

Bills

INCOME
RENT
GAS
GROCERIES
LEFT FOR BILLS

EXPENSE	DUE	AMOUNT	PAID	BALANCE LEFT

NOTES

MONTH OF

Mon	Tue	Wed	Thurs	Fri	Sat	Sun

TO DO LIST

School

Home

★ _____
★ _____
★ _____
★ _____

★ _____
★ _____
★ _____
★ _____

Schedule						
M	**T**	**W**	**TH**	**F**	**S**	**S**

Materials to Prepare	Email/Calls/Follow-Up	Reminders
● _____	● _____	● _____
● _____	● _____	● _____
● _____	● _____	● _____
● _____	● _____	● _____
● _____	● _____	● _____

Errands/Home/Personal	Upcoming To Do	Notes
● _____	● _____	● _____
● _____	● _____	● _____
● _____	● _____	● _____
● _____	● _____	● _____
● _____	● _____	● _____
● _____	● _____	● _____

Month_____

Bills

INCOME
RENT
GAS
GROCERIES
LEFT FOR BILLS

EXPENSE	DUE	AMOUNT	PAID	BALANCE LEFT

NOTES

....
....
....
....

Month_____

Bills

INCOME
RENT
GAS
GROCERIES
LEFT FOR BILLS

EXPENSE	DUE	AMOUNT	PAID	BALANCE LEFT

NOTES

....
....
....
....

MONTH OF

Mon	Tue	Wed	Thurs	Fri	Sat	Sun

TO DO LIST

School	Home

★ _____   ★ _____

★ _____   ★ _____

★ _____   ★ _____

★ _____   ★ _____

Schedule

M	**T**	**W**	**TH**	**F**	**S**	**S**

Materials to Prepare

- _____
- _____
- _____
- _____
- _____

Email/Calls/Follow-Up

- _____
- _____
- _____
- _____
- _____

Reminders

- _____
- _____
- _____
- _____
- _____

Errands/Home/Personal

- _____
- _____
- _____
- _____
- _____
- _____

Upcoming To Do

- _____
- _____
- _____
- _____
- _____
- _____

Notes

- _____
- _____
- _____
- _____
- _____
- _____

Month_____

Bills

INCOME
RENT
GAS
GROCERIES
LEFT FOR BILLS

EXPENSE	DUE	AMOUNT	PAID	BALANCE LEFT

NOTES

....

....

....

....

Month_____

Bills

INCOME
RENT
GAS
GROCERIES
LEFT FOR BILLS

EXPENSE	DUE	AMOUNT	PAID	BALANCE LEFT

NOTES

MONTH OF

Mon	Tue	Wed	Thurs	Fri	Sat	Sun

TO DO LIST

School	Home

★ _____   ★ _____

★ _____   ★ _____

★ _____   ★ _____

★ _____   ★ _____

Schedule						
M	**T**	**W**	**TH**	**F**	**S**	**S**

Materials to Prepare
- _____
- _____
- _____
- _____
- _____

Email/Calls/Follow-Up
- _____
- _____
- _____
- _____
- _____

Reminders
- _____
- _____
- _____
- _____
- _____

Errands/Home/Personal
- _____
- _____
- _____
- _____
- _____
- _____

Upcoming To Do
- _____
- _____
- _____
- _____
- _____
- _____

Notes
- _____
- _____
- _____
- _____
- _____
- _____

Month_____

Bills

INCOME
RENT
GAS
GROCERIES
LEFT FOR BILLS

EXPENSE	DUE	AMOUNT	PAID	BALANCE LEFT

NOTES

....

....

....

....

Month_____

Bills

INCOME
RENT
GAS
GROCERIES
LEFT FOR BILLS

EXPENSE	DUE	AMOUNT	PAID	BALANCE LEFT

NOTES

....

....

....

....

MONTH OF

Mon	Tue	Wed	Thurs	Fri	Sat	Sun

TO DO LIST

School	Home

★ _____   ★ _____

★ _____   ★ _____

★ _____   ★ _____

★ _____   ★ _____

Schedule						
M	**T**	**W**	**TH**	**F**	**S**	**S**

Materials to Prepare	Email/Calls/Follow-Up	Reminders
● _____	● _____	● _____
● _____	● _____	● _____
● _____	● _____	● _____
● _____	● _____	● _____
● _____	● _____	● _____

Errands/Home/Personal	Upcoming To Do	Notes
● _____	● _____	● _____
● _____	● _____	● _____
● _____	● _____	● _____
● _____	● _____	● _____
● _____	● _____	● _____
● _____	● _____	● _____

Month_____

Bills

INCOME
RENT
GAS
GROCERIES
LEFT FOR BILLS

EXPENSE	DUE	AMOUNT	PAID	BALANCE LEFT

NOTES

....
....
....
....

Month_____

Bills

INCOME
RENT
GAS
GROCERIES
LEFT FOR BILLS

EXPENSE	DUE	AMOUNT	PAID	BALANCE LEFT

NOTES

....
....
....
....

MONTH OF

Mon	Tue	Wed	Thurs	Fri	Sat	Sun

TO DO LIST

School	Home

★ _____   ★ _____

★ _____   ★ _____

★ _____   ★ _____

★ _____   ★ _____

Schedule

M	**T**	**W**	**TH**	**F**	**S**	**S**

Materials to Prepare
- _____
- _____
- _____
- _____
- _____

Email/Calls/Follow-Up
- _____
- _____
- _____
- _____
- _____

Reminders
- _____
- _____
- _____
- _____
- _____

Errands/Home/Personal
- _____
- _____
- _____
- _____
- _____
- _____

Upcoming To Do
- _____
- _____
- _____
- _____
- _____
- _____

Notes
- _____
- _____
- _____
- _____
- _____
- _____

Month_____

Bills

INCOME
RENT
GAS
GROCERIES
LEFT FOR BILLS

EXPENSE	DUE	AMOUNT	PAID	BALANCE LEFT

NOTES

....
....
....
....

Month_____

Bills

INCOME
RENT
GAS
GROCERIES
LEFT FOR BILLS

EXPENSE	DUE	AMOUNT	PAID	BALANCE LEFT

NOTES

....

....

....

....

MONTH OF

Mon	Tue	Wed	Thurs	Fri	Sat	Sun

TO DO LIST

School	Home

★ _____   ★ _____

★ _____   ★ _____

★ _____   ★ _____

★ _____   ★ _____

Schedule						
M	**T**	**W**	**TH**	**F**	**S**	**S**

Materials to Prepare	Email/Calls/Follow-Up	Reminders
● _____	● _____	● _____
● _____	● _____	● _____
● _____	● _____	● _____
● _____	● _____	● _____
● _____	● _____	● _____

Errands/Home/Personal	Upcoming To Do	Notes
● _____	● _____	● _____
● _____	● _____	● _____
● _____	● _____	● _____
● _____	● _____	● _____
● _____	● _____	● _____
● _____	● _____	● _____

Month_____

Bills

INCOME
RENT
GAS
GROCERIES
LEFT FOR BILLS

EXPENSE	DUE	AMOUNT	PAID	BALANCE LEFT

NOTES

....

....

....

....

Month_____

Bills

INCOME
RENT
GAS
GROCERIES
LEFT FOR BILLS

EXPENSE	DUE	AMOUNT	PAID	BALANCE LEFT

NOTES

....

....

....

....

MONTH OF

Mon	Tue	Wed	Thurs	Fri	Sat	Sun

TO DO LIST

School	Home

★ _____ ★ _____

★ _____ ★ _____

★ _____ ★ _____

★ _____ ★ _____

Schedule						
M	**T**	**W**	**TH**	**F**	**S**	**S**

Materials to Prepare
- _____
- _____
- _____
- _____
- _____

Email/Calls/Follow-Up
- _____
- _____
- _____
- _____
- _____

Reminders
- _____
- _____
- _____
- _____
- _____

Errands/Home/Personal
- _____
- _____
- _____
- _____
- _____
- _____

Upcoming To Do
- _____
- _____
- _____
- _____
- _____
- _____

Notes
- _____
- _____
- _____
- _____
- _____
- _____

Month_____

Bills

INCOME
RENT
GAS
GROCERIES
LEFT FOR BILLS

EXPENSE	DUE	AMOUNT	PAID	BALANCE LEFT

NOTES

....
....
....
....

Month_____

Bills

INCOME
RENT
GAS
GROCERIES
LEFT FOR BILLS

EXPENSE	DUE	AMOUNT	PAID	BALANCE LEFT

NOTES

....
....
....
....

MONTH OF

Mon	Tue	Wed	Thurs	Fri	Sat	Sun

TO DO LIST

School	Home

★ _____   ★ _____

★ _____   ★ _____

★ _____   ★ _____

★ _____   ★ _____

Schedule						
M	**T**	**W**	**TH**	**F**	**S**	**S**

Materials to Prepare

- _____
- _____
- _____
- _____
- _____

Email/Calls/Follow-Up

- _____
- _____
- _____
- _____
- _____

Reminders

- _____
- _____
- _____
- _____
- _____

Errands/Home/Personal

- _____
- _____
- _____
- _____
- _____
- _____

Upcoming To Do

- _____
- _____
- _____
- _____
- _____
- _____

Notes

- _____
- _____
- _____
- _____
- _____
- _____

Month_____

Bills

INCOME
RENT
GAS
GROCERIES
LEFT FOR BILLS

EXPENSE	DUE	AMOUNT	PAID	BALANCE LEFT

NOTES

....
....
....
....

Month_____

Bills

INCOME
RENT
GAS
GROCERIES
LEFT FOR BILLS

EXPENSE	DUE	AMOUNT	PAID	BALANCE LEFT

NOTES

....

....

....

....

MONTH OF

Mon	Tue	Wed	Thurs	Fri	Sat	Sun

TO DO LIST

School	Home

★ _____   ★ _____

★ _____   ★ _____

★ _____   ★ _____

★ _____   ★ _____

Schedule						
M	**T**	**W**	**TH**	**F**	**S**	**S**

Materials to Prepare

- _____
- _____
- _____
- _____
- _____

Email/Calls/Follow-Up

- _____
- _____
- _____
- _____
- _____

Reminders

- _____
- _____
- _____
- _____
- _____

Errands/Home/Personal

- _____
- _____
- _____
- _____
- _____
- _____

Upcoming To Do

- _____
- _____
- _____
- _____
- _____
- _____

Notes

- _____
- _____
- _____
- _____
- _____

Month_____

Bills

INCOME
RENT
GAS
GROCERIES
LEFT FOR BILLS

EXPENSE	DUE	AMOUNT	PAID	BALANCE LEFT

NOTES

....

....

....

....

Month_____

Bills

INCOME
RENT
GAS
GROCERIES
LEFT FOR BILLS

EXPENSE	DUE	AMOUNT	PAID	BALANCE LEFT

NOTES

....
....
....
....

MONTH OF

Mon	Tue	Wed	Thurs	Fri	Sat	Sun

TO DO LIST

School	Home

★ _____   ★ _____

★ _____   ★ _____

★ _____   ★ _____

★ _____   ★ _____

Schedule

M	**T**	**W**	**TH**	**F**	**S**	**S**

Materials to Prepare
- _____
- _____
- _____
- _____
- _____

Email/Calls/Follow-Up
- _____
- _____
- _____
- _____
- _____

Reminders
- _____
- _____
- _____
- _____
- _____

Errands/Home/Personal
- _____
- _____
- _____
- _____
- _____
- _____

Upcoming To Do
- _____
- _____
- _____
- _____
- _____
- _____

Notes
- _____
- _____
- _____
- _____
- _____
- _____

Month_____

Bills

INCOME
RENT
GAS
GROCERIES
LEFT FOR BILLS

EXPENSE	DUE	AMOUNT	PAID	BALANCE LEFT

NOTES

....
....
....
....

Month_____

Bills

INCOME
RENT
GAS
GROCERIES
LEFT FOR BILLS

EXPENSE	DUE	AMOUNT	PAID	BALANCE LEFT

NOTES

....
....
....
....

MONTH OF

Mon	Tue	Wed	Thurs	Fri	Sat	Sun

TO DO LIST

School

★ _____

★ _____

★ _____

★ _____

Home

★ _____

★ _____

★ _____

★ _____

Schedule						
M	**T**	**W**	**TH**	**F**	**S**	**S**

Materials to Prepare

- _____
- _____
- _____
- _____
- _____

Email/Calls/Follow-Up

- _____
- _____
- _____
- _____
- _____

Reminders

- _____
- _____
- _____
- _____
- _____

Errands/Home/Personal

- _____
- _____
- _____
- _____
- _____
- _____

Upcoming To Do

- _____
- _____
- _____
- _____
- _____
- _____

Notes

- _____
- _____
- _____
- _____
- _____
- _____

Month_____

Bills

INCOME
RENT
GAS
GROCERIES
LEFT FOR BILLS

EXPENSE	DUE	AMOUNT	PAID	BALANCE LEFT

NOTES

....
....
....
....

Month_____

Bills

INCOME
RENT
GAS
GROCERIES
LEFT FOR BILLS

EXPENSE	DUE	AMOUNT	PAID	BALANCE LEFT

NOTES

....
....
....
....

MONTH OF

Mon	Tue	Wed	Thurs	Fri	Sat	Sun

TO DO LIST

School	Home

★ _____   ★ _____

★ _____   ★ _____

★ _____   ★ _____

★ _____   ★ _____

Schedule

M	T	W	TH	F	S	S

Materials to Prepare
- _____
- _____
- _____
- _____
- _____

Email/Calls/Follow-Up
- _____
- _____
- _____
- _____
- _____

Reminders
- _____
- _____
- _____
- _____
- _____

Errands/Home/Personal
- _____
- _____
- _____
- _____
- _____
- _____

Upcoming To Do
- _____
- _____
- _____
- _____
- _____
- _____

Notes
- _____
- _____
- _____
- _____
- _____
- _____

Month_____

Bills

INCOME
RENT
GAS
GROCERIES
LEFT FOR BILLS

EXPENSE	DUE	AMOUNT	PAID	BALANCE LEFT

NOTES

....
....
....
....

Month_____

$\mathcal{B}ills$

INCOME
RENT
GAS
GROCERIES
LEFT FOR BILLS

EXPENSE	DUE	AMOUNT	PAID	BALANCE LEFT

NOTES

....
....
....
....

MONTH OF

Mon	Tue	Wed	Thurs	Fri	Sat	Sun

TO DO LIST

School	Home

★ _____   ★ _____

★ _____   ★ _____

★ _____   ★ _____

★ _____   ★ _____

Schedule						
M	**T**	**W**	**TH**	**F**	**S**	**S**

Materials to Prepare

- _____
- _____
- _____
- _____
- _____

Email/Calls/Follow-Up

- _____
- _____
- _____
- _____
- _____

Reminders

- _____
- _____
- _____
- _____
- _____

Errands/Home/Personal

- _____
- _____
- _____
- _____
- _____

Upcoming To Do

- _____
- _____
- _____
- _____
- _____

Notes

- _____
- _____
- _____
- _____
- _____

Month_____

Bills

INCOME
RENT
GAS
GROCERIES
LEFT FOR BILLS

EXPENSE	DUE	AMOUNT	PAID	BALANCE LEFT

NOTES

....
....
....
....

Month_____

Bills

INCOME
RENT
GAS
GROCERIES
LEFT FOR BILLS

EXPENSE	DUE	AMOUNT	PAID	BALANCE LEFT

NOTES

....
....
....
....

MONTH OF

Mon	Tue	Wed	Thurs	Fri	Sat	Sun

TO DO LIST

School	Home

★ _____   ★ _____

★ _____   ★ _____

★ _____   ★ _____

★ _____   ★ _____

Schedule

M	T	W	TH	F	S	S

Materials to Prepare

- _____
- _____
- _____
- _____
- _____

Email/Calls/Follow-Up

- _____
- _____
- _____
- _____
- _____

Reminders

- _____
- _____
- _____
- _____
- _____

Errands/Home/Personal

- _____
- _____
- _____
- _____
- _____
- _____

Upcoming To Do

- _____
- _____
- _____
- _____
- _____
- _____

Notes

- _____
- _____
- _____
- _____
- _____
- _____

Month_____

Bills

INCOME
RENT
GAS
GROCERIES
LEFT FOR BILLS

EXPENSE	DUE	AMOUNT	PAID	BALANCE LEFT

NOTES

....

....

....

....

Month_____

Bills

INCOME
RENT
GAS
GROCERIES
LEFT FOR BILLS

EXPENSE	DUE	AMOUNT	PAID	BALANCE LEFT

NOTES
....
....
....
....

MONTH OF

Mon	Tue	Wed	Thurs	Fri	Sat	Sun

TO DO LIST

School	Home

★ _____   ★ _____

★ _____   ★ _____

★ _____   ★ _____

★ _____   ★ _____

Schedule						
M	**T**	**W**	**TH**	**F**	**S**	**S**

Materials to Prepare

- _____
- _____
- _____
- _____
- _____

Email/Calls/Follow-Up

- _____
- _____
- _____
- _____
- _____

Reminders

- _____
- _____
- _____
- _____
- _____

Errands/Home/Personal

- _____
- _____
- _____
- _____
- _____
- _____

Upcoming To Do

- _____
- _____
- _____
- _____
- _____
- _____

Notes

- _____
- _____
- _____
- _____
- _____
- _____

Month_____

Bills

INCOME
RENT
GAS
GROCERIES
LEFT FOR BILLS

EXPENSE	DUE	AMOUNT	PAID	BALANCE LEFT

NOTES

....
....
....
....

Month_____

Bills

INCOME
RENT
GAS
GROCERIES
LEFT FOR BILLS

EXPENSE	DUE	AMOUNT	PAID	BALANCE LEFT

NOTES

....
....
....
....

MONTH OF

Mon	Tue	Wed	Thurs	Fri	Sat	Sun

TO DO LIST

School	Home

★ _____   ★ _____

★ _____   ★ _____

★ _____   ★ _____

★ _____   ★ _____

Schedule						
M	**T**	**W**	**TH**	**F**	**S**	**S**

Materials to Prepare

- _____
- _____
- _____
- _____
- _____

Email/Calls/Follow-Up

- _____
- _____
- _____
- _____
- _____

Reminders

- _____
- _____
- _____
- _____
- _____

Errands/Home/Personal

- _____
- _____
- _____
- _____
- _____
- _____

Upcoming To Do

- _____
- _____
- _____
- _____
- _____
- _____

Notes

- _____
- _____
- _____
- _____
- _____
- _____

Month_____

Bills

INCOME
RENT
GAS
GROCERIES
LEFT FOR BILLS

EXPENSE	DUE	AMOUNT	PAID	BALANCE LEFT

NOTES

....

....

....

....

Month_____

Bills

INCOME
RENT
GAS
GROCERIES
LEFT FOR BILLS

EXPENSE	DUE	AMOUNT	PAID	BALANCE LEFT

NOTES

....
....
....
....

MONTH OF

Mon	Tue	Wed	Thurs	Fri	Sat	Sun

TO DO LIST

School	Home

★ _____   ★ _____

★ _____   ★ _____

★ _____   ★ _____

★ _____   ★ _____

Schedule

M	T	W	TH	F	S	S

Materials to Prepare
- _____
- _____
- _____
- _____
- _____

Email/Calls/Follow-Up
- _____
- _____
- _____
- _____
- _____

Reminders
- _____
- _____
- _____
- _____
- _____

Errands/Home/Personal
- _____
- _____
- _____
- _____
- _____
- _____

Upcoming To Do
- _____
- _____
- _____
- _____
- _____
- _____

Notes
- _____
- _____
- _____
- _____
- _____
- _____

Month_____

Bills

INCOME
RENT
GAS
GROCERIES
LEFT FOR BILLS

EXPENSE	DUE	AMOUNT	PAID	BALANCE LEFT

NOTES

....
....
....
....

Month_____

Bills

INCOME
RENT
GAS
GROCERIES
LEFT FOR BILLS

EXPENSE	DUE	AMOUNT	PAID	BALANCE LEFT

NOTES

....
....
....
....

MONTH OF

Mon	Tue	Wed	Thurs	Fri	Sat	Sun

TO DO LIST

School

★ _____

★ _____

★ _____

★ _____

Home

★ _____

★ _____

★ _____

★ _____

Schedule

M	**T**	**W**	**TH**	**F**	**S**	**S**

Materials to Prepare

- _____
- _____
- _____
- _____
- _____

Email/Calls/Follow-Up

- _____
- _____
- _____
- _____
- _____

Reminders

- _____
- _____
- _____
- _____
- _____

Errands/Home/Personal

- _____
- _____
- _____
- _____
- _____
- _____

Upcoming To Do

- _____
- _____
- _____
- _____
- _____
- _____

Notes

- _____
- _____
- _____
- _____
- _____
- _____

Month_____

Bills

INCOME
RENT
GAS
GROCERIES
LEFT FOR BILLS

EXPENSE	DUE	AMOUNT	PAID	BALANCE LEFT

NOTES

....
....
....
....

Month_____

Bills

INCOME
RENT
GAS
GROCERIES
LEFT FOR BILLS

EXPENSE	DUE	AMOUNT	PAID	BALANCE LEFT

NOTES

....

....

....

....

MONTH OF

Mon	Tue	Wed	Thurs	Fri	Sat	Sun

TO DO LIST

School

★ _____

★ _____

★ _____

★ _____

Home

★ _____

★ _____

★ _____

★ _____

Schedule						
M	**T**	**W**	**TH**	**F**	**S**	**S**

Materials to Prepare

● _____
● _____
● _____
● _____
● _____

Email/Calls/Follow-Up

● _____
● _____
● _____
● _____
● _____

Reminders

● _____
● _____
● _____
● _____
● _____

Errands/Home/Personal

● _____
● _____
● _____
● _____
● _____
● _____

Upcoming To Do

● _____
● _____
● _____
● _____
● _____
● _____

Notes

● _____
● _____
● _____
● _____
● _____
● _____

Month_____

Bills

INCOME
RENT
GAS
GROCERIES
LEFT FOR BILLS

EXPENSE	DUE	AMOUNT	PAID	BALANCE LEFT

NOTES

....

....

....

....

Month_____

Bills

INCOME
RENT
GAS
GROCERIES
LEFT FOR BILLS

EXPENSE	DUE	AMOUNT	PAID	BALANCE LEFT

NOTES

....
....
....
....

MONTH OF

Mon	Tue	Wed	Thurs	Fri	Sat	Sun

TO DO LIST

School	Home

★ _____   ★ _____

★ _____   ★ _____

★ _____   ★ _____

★ _____   ★ _____

Schedule						
M	**T**	**W**	**TH**	**F**	**S**	**S**

Materials to Prepare

- _____
- _____
- _____
- _____
- _____

Email/Calls/Follow-Up

- _____
- _____
- _____
- _____
- _____

Reminders

- _____
- _____
- _____
- _____
- _____

Errands/Home/Personal

- _____
- _____
- _____
- _____
- _____
- _____

Upcoming To Do

- _____
- _____
- _____
- _____
- _____
- _____

Notes

- _____
- _____
- _____
- _____
- _____
- _____

Month_____

Bills

INCOME
RENT
GAS
GROCERIES
LEFT FOR BILLS

EXPENSE	DUE	AMOUNT	PAID	BALANCE LEFT

NOTES
....
....
....
....

Month_____

Bills

INCOME
RENT
GAS
GROCERIES
LEFT FOR BILLS

EXPENSE	DUE	AMOUNT	PAID	BALANCE LEFT

NOTES

....

....

....

....

www.ingramcontent.com/pod-product-compliance
Lightning Source LLC
Chambersburg PA
CBHW081338090426
42737CB00017B/3193